HERBS FOR HORSES

by

Jenny Morgan

with an Introduction by
Graham Wheeler, BVSc, BSc, PhD, MRCVS

Illustrations by

Carole Vincer

KENILWORTH PRESS

First published in Great Britain by
The Kenilworth Press Limited,
Addington, Buckingham, MK18 2JR

© The Kenilworth Press Limited 1993
Reprinted 1994, 1996, 1998

British Library Cataloguing in Publication Data
A catalogue record for this book is available from the British Library.

ISBN 1-872082-46-7

Typeset by Kenilworth Press

Printed in Great Britain by Westway Offset, Wembley

CONTENTS ■ ■ ■ ■ ■ ■ ■ ■ ■ ■ ■ ■

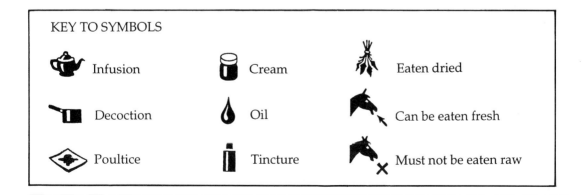

KEY TO SYMBOLS

Infusion   Cream   Eaten dried

Decoction   Oil   Can be eaten fresh

Poultice   Tincture   Must not be eaten raw

Introduction ■ ■ ■ ■ ■ ■ ■ ■ ■ ■ ■ ■ ■ ■

by Graham Wheeler, Veterinary Surgeon

Years ago, when horses roamed free, their diet included a good proportion of the herbs which are included in today's dried herbal mixtures. They would have been ingested fresh as part of normal grazing and when horses were ill, they instinctively sought out the herbs which they knew would help them. This 'dowsing' ability has been greatly reduced by domestication and our horses have delegated responsibility for their health to us.

Until relatively recently, the veterinary surgeon played very little part in this care. The groom or farmer would have an armoury of remedies, almost exclusively herbal, with which to treat his own horses. Knowledge of these remedies was largely passed down by word of mouth, although more educated people might have consulted a human herbal in search of a remedy. This is not altogether a safe practice, even today, because many human herbals list plants which, whilst relatively safe for human beings, are poisonous for horses, who have different digestive, metabolic and biological mechanisms.

With the advent of multi-national drug companies and a swing towards sophisticated veterinary medicine, horse owners moved away from more 'old-fashioned' treatments – and indeed many owners have reason to be grateful for modern drugs and the skills of the veterinary surgeon. However, close on the heels of the human alternative medicine revolution is a clear shift in favour of natural remedies for animals, both in prevention and cures.

Although in some emergencies, such as a severe wound or other acute condition, herbal medicine is not the first or best therapy, herbs can, nevertheless, be very efficient in maintaining health, correcting minor problems and supporting recovery in serious illness. This book aims to give the horse owner an introduction to the use of simple and effective herbs, most of which are easily grown or can be found growing wild. Collection of herbs from the wild should, however, be carried out with care and responsibility for conservation. Also included is useful information on some of the herbs most commonly found in proprietary mixes, so a more enlightened choice can be made when buying your herbs this way.

Dr Graham Wheeler, BVSc, BSc, PhD, MRCVS

■ ■

Using herbs

Most horse owners will buy a proprietary herbal mix which has been specially blended for a particular problem. However, it is possible to blend your own mixes, using herbs which you have gathered and dried yourself. It is also very easy to make infusions and decoctions for internal and external use and to blend your own creams. These simple natural remedies are far more cost-effective than 'bought' preparations. Indeed, many very common and well-known plants provide safe and effective remedies. You will not only save money, but also have the satisfaction of using a remedy which has been proven by centuries of use rather than by trials on laboratory animals.

For the competition horse, it is well worth remembering that the herbs mentioned in this book should not contain any banned substance when fed at the recommended levels and therefore should not need to be discontinued at the time of competition. However, if you are in any doubt, you should seek qualified advice.

Always take care to pick your herbs from a 'clean' source, rather than somewhere such as the roadside. If you are drying them for winter use, make sure that they are completely dry before storage, to avoid contamination by moulds. Do not attempt to use any plant if you are not completely sure of its identification. Do not use more than the recommended amount.

Most important – always consult your veterinary surgeon if you are in any doubt.

Garlic

(Allium sativum)

This well-known plant, of which the bulb is used, is widely cultivated. The valuable properties of garlic have been recognised for at least 5,000 years.

Garlic has several actions: antibiotic, expectorant, antihistamine, and anti-parasitic. It has been shown, in human research trials, to reduce blood pressure and blood cholesterol levels. Strong aromatic compounds are excreted through the skin and act as a fly repellent.

The uses of garlic are many. This herb is very beneficial for horses with allergic coughing and bronchitis. It is a useful addition to antibiotic treatments in cases of infection. The blood-cleansing action makes regular use of garlic a good preventative measure for horses prone to laminitis, arthritic problems, sweet itch and skin problems. A poultice of crushed fresh cloves can be used for infected or dirty wounds.

Although garlic alone cannot control worms, regular use does help to keep down the worm population.

Garlic can be fed fresh at the rate of up to five cloves per day, but most horses prefer a proprietary powder, mixed into the feed at a rate of up to 50g per day.

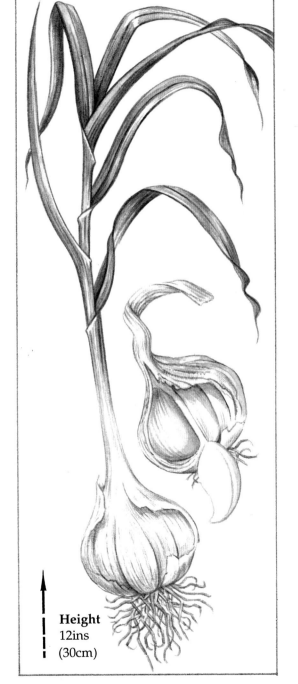

Height
12ins
(30cm)

Stinging nettle

(Urtica dioica)

A well-known plant growing almost everywhere. Nettles are a valuable food and medicine, being rich in minerals, particularly iron, calcium and potassium.

The vitamin C content of the plant ensures absorption of iron, making nettles a useful addition to veterinary treatment, in anaemia.

Historically used as a spring tonic, the 'cleansing' effect is useful in sweet itch and other skin conditions, laminitis, arthritis and rheumatism. A decoction of the root can be used internally or externally to improve the condition of mane, tail and coat. Nettles are known to be useful in cases of internal haemorrhage.

Broodmares can benefit from nettles, after foaling, to improve their milk flow and boost their levels of iron and other minerals.

Although horses do not seem to eat growing nettles, the plants are easily gathered (wearing gloves!), when flowering, and dried, to feed at the rate of up to 50g per day.

Height
3 – 6ft
(90 – 180cm)

Dandelion

(Taraxacum officinale)

A common plant, often regarded as a weed. The name comes from the French *dent de lion*, meaning lion's tooth, referring to the shape of the leaves.

Most horses love dandelions, relishing the leaves and flowers. Dandelion leaves contain over 4% potassium (on a dry matter basis). They stimulate excretion of water from the body via the kidneys (i.e. are diuretic) and also act as a liver and digestive tonic. Dandelion cleanses the blood, making it useful in laminitis, skin diseases and rheumatism.

The white 'sap' from the broken stalks is thought to be a cure for warts. It should be applied daily (but not to bleeding warts, which should be seen by the vet).

Dandelion is a 'bitter' and therefore encourages appetite and improves digestion. It is also a mild laxative. A few fresh dandelion leaves are a valuable addition to the feed of the convalescent horse for these reasons.

Dandelions can be dried for winter use – although it is usually possible to find a few leaves growing even in the middle of winter. They should be fed at the rate of up to 50g (dried weight), or a good double handful or fresh leaves per day.

Height
up to 1ft (30cm)

Fenugreek

(Trigonella foenum-graecum)

The Latin name of this herb means 'Greek hay' and emphasises its long-time use as a fodder crop. The seeds of this herb are the most dramatic body and hoof conditioner and appetizer, putting on flesh and making the coat shine, in a very short time. It is also a uterine stimulant and should not be used during pregnancy. Fenugreek, however, is most useful for the nursing mare, improving both her milk flow and her condition after foaling.

Fenugreek can be added to garlic for horses with respiratory problems. The dried, crushed seeds can be used as a poultice for rheumatic pains and also to remove thorns.

Although it is possible to grow fenugreek yourself, it is the seeds which are usually used and therefore it is easier to buy a proprietary brand in powder form and feed at the recommended rate (usually around 75g per day).

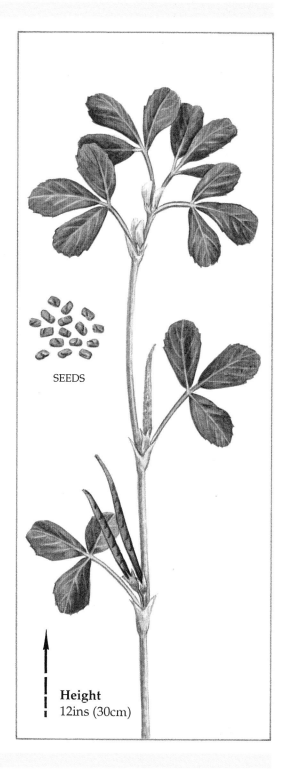

SEEDS

Height
12ins (30cm)

Red clover

(Trifolium pratense)

A meadow plant, cultivated in the past as a fodder crop mainly for cattle. It used to be thought that if clover leaves were seen to be trembling, it was a sign of imminent storm or tempest!

Clover flower heads are used in several ways. They can be fed to clean the blood in skin complaints, such as sweet itch.

Another use is in bronchitis and allied complaints. For this they can either be fed fresh or dried or made into a simple syrup, by boiling with sugar and water. When cool, this can be placed on the tongue with a wooden spoon.

The fresh flowers can be crushed and rubbed onto insect bites, utilising the methyl salicitate in this herb. The flower heads can also be infused to bathe sweet itch, mud fever and other skin conditions.

In the 1930s red clover was a popular cancer remedy. Although there is little scientific evidence to prove effectiveness, it could well be worth feeding this herb to white horses with melanoma.

The flowers are easily dried, shaking thoroughly first to remove insects. They should be fed at the rate of up to 50g per day.

Height
20ins (50cm)

Kelp, seaweed

(Fucus vesiculosus)

In herbals, kelp refers to the plant *Fucus vesiculosus* (commonly known as Bladderwrack) and also to other species of the family Fucaceae. Bladderwrack is easily identified by its spherical air vesicles (as shown right). If you are lucky enough to live by an unpolluted beach, you can gather your own, but you must be absolutely sure of the identity of the plant. All seaweed is at risk from heavy metal contamination, including cadmium, mercury and arsenic, so it is probably better to purchase kelp in a powder form.

Being rich in minerals, including calcium, iodine and potassium, it is a useful supplement for horses who are or have been on poor grazing. Seaweed is thought to improve arthritic and rheumatic conditions and certainly, if the whole fresh plant is available, a decoction can be made to use as a cold compress on the joints. A tincture (sometimes known as Thalli) can also be used (20ml of tincture to 500ml of water) to soak the compress. Seaweed is a good coat and hoof conditioner and helps to promote the loss of winter coat.

Whether you are feeding fresh seaweed or that which you have dried yourself, you should not use more than 50g per day. Kelp is widely available as a comercially dried product and should be fed according to the manufacturers instructions.

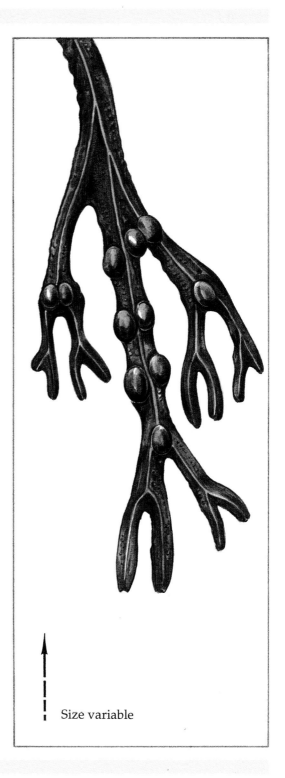

Size variable

Common ailments chart

DANDRUFF AND HAIR LOSS
EXTERNAL: Wash with an infusion of **nettle** and **rosemary**.
INTERNAL: **Nettle, garlic, kelp. Fenugreek** and **linseed** are both good coat conditioners.

SWEET ITCH
EXTERNAL: Bathe affected areas with a **mint** infusio
Allow this to dry and then put **marigold cream** or
any particularly sore areas.
INTERNAL: Start feeding **garlic**, **nettle** and **dandelic**
well before itching starts. If pony starts rubbing, a
chamomile and use external remedies as above.

EYE INFECTIONS
EXTERNAL: Bathe with **eyebright** infusion.
INTERNAL: **Garlic.**

INSECT BITES AND STINGS
EXTERNAL: Place fresh **onion** on stings for rapid relief. Stings can also be rubbed with a handful of fresh **mint. Witch hazel** is useful too.

BRIDLE INJURIES AND SADDLE SORES
EXTERNAL: Wash with an infusion of **marigold** and **St John's wort**. Dry thoroughly. When dry gently massage with **comfrey ointment**. Check saddlery for correct fitting.

THRUSH
EXTERNAL: Clean hoofs out thoroughly every day with warm water containing a few drops of **tea tree oil**. Apply neat **tea tree oil** to worst affected areas. Keep clean and dry if possible.

BRUSHING
EXTERNAL: Use **marigold cream** on any wounds which may occur. Check for faulty shoeing.

SANDCRACK AND POOR HOOF CONDITION
EXTERNAL: **Linseed oil** or good **hoof oil** should be painted on regularly.
INTERNAL: **Rosehips** contain natural biotin which encourages strong growth. Also feed **kelp** and **fenugreek**.

BRONCHITIS AND ALLERGIC COUGH
EXTERNAL: Steam inhalation of **eucalyptus oil**. For allergic cough use a steam inhalation of fresh **yarrow**. Put a few dro of **eucalyptus oil** (or a handful of **yarrow leaves**) on a coupl handfuls of good hay in the bottom of a bucket. Pour on boi water. Hold the bucket as near the horse's nostrils as he wil allow.
INTERNAL: **Garlic, fenugreek, red clover**. Also **coltsfoot syru** (buy a preparation for human use).

LAMINITIS
INTERNAL: **Garlic, nettle, dandelion**, as a preventative.

Always seek veterinary advice if you suspect laminitis.

DERMATITIS, RAIN SCALD, MUD FEVER

EXTERNAL: Wash with an infusion of **marigold**, with a few drops of **tea tree oil** added. Dry thoroughly. For severe cases use a poultice of **marigold petals**.
INTERNAL: **Garlic, nettle**.

WOUNDS AND BLEEDING

Serious wounds always require veterinary attention.
EXTERNAL: Wash with an infusion of **marigold** or **St John's wort**. Allow to dry, then apply **marigold cream**. If infected, use **tea tree oil**. Crushed **garlic cloves** or fresh **yarrow leaves** can be used as a poultice to stop bleeding, particularly as a first aid measure until the vet arrives. *Any wound which does not stop bleeding very quickly needs expert attention.*
INTERNAL: **Garlic**.

SMALL FRACTURES

EXTERNAL: For fractures such as of the splint bone, point of hock or facial bones, *after veterinary diagnosis*, apply a **comfrey** poultice regularly. To relieve swelling, a cold **witch hazel** compress should be applied gently.

LOSS OF CONDITION

Any loss of condition for an unknown reason should be investigated by the vet.
EXTERNAL: Use **nettle** and **rosemary** infusion as a final rinse when bathing your horse or brush it in when grooming to improve mane, tail and coat.
INTERNAL: **Fenugreek, kelp, linseed, alfalfa**.

RHEUMATISM AND ARTHRITIS

EXTERNAL: Fresh **cabbage** can be used as a poultice for joints.
INTERNAL: Feed **garlic, linseed, golden rod** or a proprietary preparation containing **devil's claw**.

ANAEMIA

INTERNAL: *This should always be treated by a vet*, but dried **nettles** do contain iron, so make a useful adjunct to conventional veterinary treatment.

BRUISING, SPRAINS AND STRAINS

EXTERNAL: Use a cold **witch hazel** poultice to reduce swelling and inflammation, then use **comfrey** or **St John's wort oil** (see page 24). A mixture of **yarrow oil** and **St John's wort oil** can be rubbed into inflamed joints.

LOSS OF APPETITE

INTERNAL: **Mint, fenugreek, dandelion. Carrots** and an infusion of **oats** (oat tea) are also useful. Dried **hops** can be fed for two or three days.

COLIC

Do not attempt to treat all but the very mildest colic, without veterinary help.
INTERNAL: As a first aid measure, **chamomile tea**. This should be cooled to lukewarm and either offered as a drink or fed on a small amount of bran. For horses prone to colic give **fenugreek** and **mint** regularly.

STRESS AND NERVOUS CONDITIONS

EXTERNAL: Use a mixture of **lavender** and **neroli** oils (see page 24) rubbed into your hands when handling a nervous horse. This same mixture can also be rubbed into his forelock, so that he can inhale the calming aroma.
INTERNAL: **Chamomile, valerian**. Also **hops** - but do not feed for more than a few days at a time.

IMPORTANT NOTE: Please refer to the descriptions of the individual herbs for usage quantities and to page 24 for details of preparation. It is quite in order to feed two or more herbs at once.

Flax, linseed

(Linum usitatissimum)

Although unknown in the wild, this plant has been cultivated since at least 5,000 BC. It is best known for the use of its fibres for cloth, but both the seeds and the oil obtained from them are useful in herbal medicine.

The oil is a mild laxative and has an anti-inflammatory effect on gastritis. It also soothes sore throats connected with respiratory infections.

A poultice of the crushed seeds can be used to foment abscesses.

Linseed is a valuable feed for old horses with arthritis. It helps to maintain condition and also has a slight anti-inflammatory effect.

The seeds contain 30 - 40% oil and around 25% protein, making them an excellent conditioner for the skin and coat and overall condition. They also contain prussic acid (a poison) so must be boiled for at least two hours before feeding. **Never** feed the seeds without boiling. The boiled seeds form a jelly-like mass. Linseed jelly makes a good appetiser for a fussy feeder. The oil of linseed has been found to help leach toxic heavy metals from the body of the animal.

If feeding linseed oil, do remember that too large a dose will act as a purgative. Either follow the directions on the bottle or give 30ml day.

LINSEED

Height
12 – 50ins
(30 – 130cm)

Rosehips

(Rosa rugosa, R. canina)

Rosa rugosa is the variety most commonly used for rose hedging. *Rosa canina* is the wild dog rose, so called because it used to be thought that this plant could cure a bite from a mad dog.

Rosehips are usually fed to horses for their biotin content. Biotin promotes healthy hoof growth. They are also a valuable source of vitamins C, E and K, and nicotinamide.

In Chinese herbal medicine rosehips are used as a liver tonic, and could therefore be useful for the horse with a liver-based disease such as laminitis.

Use up to 35g per day of dried hips, which should be minced or ground before feeding.

Rosa canina

Height
up to
10ft (3m)

ROSE HIPS

Raspberry

(Rubus idaeus)

This soft fruit favourite is also a valuable medicinal plant. If taken during late pregnancy (last eight weeks) and after foaling, the leaves have a beneficial effect by toning pelvic and uterine muscles as well as enhancing milk production. This remedy should not, however, be used during early pregnancy. The leaves can also be used for their cleansing effect in rheumatic conditions.

Use up to 50g of dried or 75g of fresh leaves per day.

Height
3 – 5ft
(90 – 150cm)

Mint

(Mentha piperita, M. spicata)

Both *piperita* (peppermint) and *spicata* (spearmint) are useful common garden varieties of this herb. Peppermint is rather stronger than spearmint. Mint is best known as a flavouring and an appetiser. This herb relaxes the muscles of the digestive tract and it is therefore useful to add a small (20g) daily dose of mint to the feed of horses who are prone to colic. It also encourages fussy feeders.

Peppermint oil contains menthol which has anti-fungal properties and is therefore useful against ringworm. Use 2-3 drops in 10ml of water. The oil can also be diluted – 10 drops to 25ml of sunflower oil – and used to 'cool' inflamed joints.

Mint is easily dried for winter use, but because most of the activity of mint is related to its content of so-called volatile oils, the efficacy of dried mint is rather low when compared to that of fresh mint. Dried mint should be fed at the rate of 50g per day. Fresh mint should be chopped up and fed at the rate of 50g per day.

When encouraging a fussy feeder, the herb should be sprinkled on top of the feed after it has been mixed.

Fresh mint can be rubbed on insect bites and stings. An infusion of mint can be used to cool the itching of sweet itch.

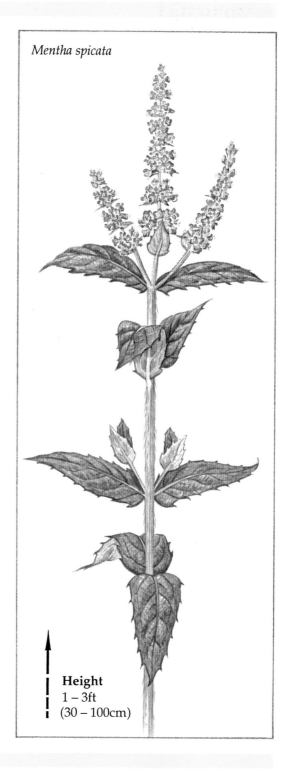

Mentha spicata

Height
1 – 3ft
(30 – 100cm)

16

Marigold

(Calendula officinalis)

A very useful plant indeed, often known as 'pot' marigold. This is a well-known and popular cottage-garden plant and should be grown in every horse owner's garden!

The petals are used for a variety of conditions. Their actions include anti-fungal, anti-bacterial, anti-inflammatory and wound healing amongst others. It is a most important herb for liver problems and should always be included in the treatment of such disorders. It is also a useful herb for digestive problems.

An infusion can be used for fungal conditions such as thrush and ringworm, and for washing wounds.

Marigold cream is very easy to make (follow the instructions on page 24) and is excellent for all wounds and skin problems. It has the effect of softening skin and scabs in mud fever. The anti-bacterial effect can then promote recovery.

Dry, without overheating, and store only the petals of the flowers. If feeding, use 30g per day.

Height
20ins (50cm)

Chamomile

(Matricaria chamomilla,
Chamaemelum nobile)

Matricaria chamomilla is sometimes known as German chamomile. Also available is *Chamaemelum nobile* or Russian chamomile. Both have similar properties.

Chamomile is most often used for horses for its sedative properties. It can safely be fed before competition to calm nerves, without affecting performance. It is not a prohibited substance. Many riders also benefit from a cup of chamomile tea to soothe pre-competition nerves! It is extremely useful for horses which are prone to 'nervous' colic, and can be fed regularly to horses who are of this disposition.

Ointment or cream containing chamomile is very useful for sweet itch and other dermatitis. A compress can be used for a mare with a sore udder.

The flowers are used, either dried or fresh, at the rate of up to 50g per day. Do not exceed the stated dose.

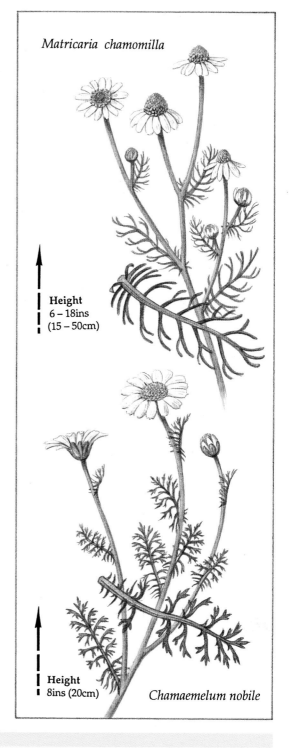

Matricaria chamomilla

Height
6 – 18ins
(15 – 50cm)

Height
8ins (20cm)

Chamaemelum nobile

Comfrey

(Symphytum officinale)

Comfrey is a common native herb, often found growing in pasture. It is without doubt the most controversial herb in regular use for horses. The reason for the controversy is the presence of pyrrolizidine alkaloids in some cultivars of comfrey, which may cause cancer. Since it is possible to find other, safer herbs to use internally, and since comfrey has been banned for human consumption, it is better restricted to external use only.

As a healing plant for external use it is remarkable. The reason for this is a substance called allantoin, which encourages cell growth, and which is easily absorbed through the skin. Fresh or dried leaves can be used either as a poultice, compress or cream for wounds. A puree of fresh leaves can be used as a poultice for minor fractures, for example of the splint bone. Ointment or oil can be rubbed into arthritic joints, sprains and tendon injuries.

Do not use on dirty wounds as the accelerated rate of wound healing could trap foreign material at the wound site.

FLOWERS: PALE YELLOW
TO PURPLE AND VIOLET

Height
30ins (80cm)

Other useful herbs

The herbs on these pages are often found in proprietary mixes. Please follow the instructions on the packaging carefully.

Coltsfoot
(Tussilago farfara)
Often found in cough preparations. It has a soothing effect on dry coughs. Coltsfoot has been shown to contain hepatoxic alkaloids similar to those found in comfrey, which may pose potential risks during long-term use. It is possible to give coltsfoot syrup, sold for human use, to horses, with good effect. Use 30ml, either squirted into the mouth from a plastic syringe, or put on top of feed.

Horseradish
(Cochlearia armoracia)
The word 'horse' does not necessarily mean it is good for horses: it is a corruption of the word 'coarse'. Nevertheless the root makes a very good, occasional, warming poultice to enhance blood flow around sprains and strains. Horseradish is also found in cough preparations.

Devil's claw
(Harpogophytum procumbens)
An African plant (but, as dried devil's claw, obtainable all over the world) with proven anti-inflammatory and pain-relieving properties. It is often found in arthritis remedies and is very useful for 'arthritic' riders too! Do not use during pregnancy.

Golden rod
(Solidago virgaurea)
Found mostly in arthritis and rheumatism mixes. This herb is also useful for kidney and bladder infections.

Hops
(Humulus lupulus)
The recently dried flowers of this plant are a well-known sedative, but should be used with caution. The hormonal properties of hops mean that they are better avoided for broodmares and stallions. Hops make a good bitter tonic for the fractious horse who fails to thrive.

Valerian
(Valeriana officinalis)
A potent tranquilliser, nearly always found in proprietary 'calming' mixtures. This herb can also be useful for very mild colic, particularly in the horse whose digestion is affected by competition nerves. Never exceed the stated dose, and do not use regularly for prolonged periods.

Alfalfa
(Medicago sativa)
Also known as lucerne. Widely grown as a fodder crop. This herb contains 16% protein and is high in vitamins and minerals and is therefore useful for putting on condition.

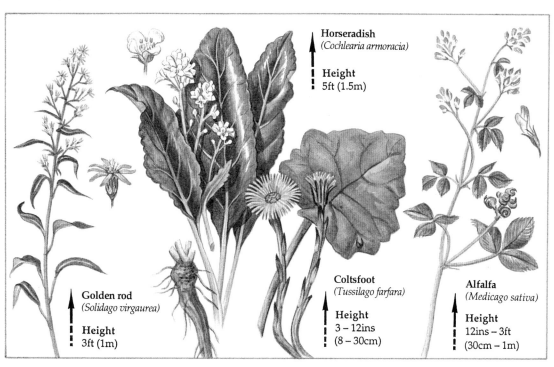

Horseradish
(Cochlearia armoracia)

Height
5ft (1.5m)

Golden rod
(Solidago virgaurea)

Height
3ft (1m)

Coltsfoot
(Tussilago farfara)

Height
3 – 12ins
(8 – 30cm)

Alfalfa
(Medicago sativa)

Height
12ins – 3ft
(30cm – 1m)

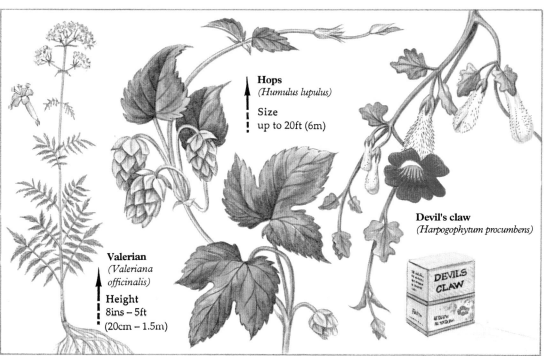

Hops
(Humulus lupulus)

Size
up to 20ft (6m)

Devil's claw
(Harpogophytum procumbens)

DEVILS
CLAW

Valerian
*(Valeriana
officinalis)*

Height
8ins – 5ft
(20cm – 1.5m)

Useful herbs for external use

These herbs are suitable for external use only.

Eyebright

*(Euphrasia officinalis
or E. rostkoviana)*
This is a most useful herb for bathing eyes, particularly when they have been irritated by flies. A European native, but tincture or dried varieties are obtainable everywhere. Use the dried herb for an infusion or buy a tincture and dilute according to the instructions.

Yarrow

(Achillea millefolium)
Yarrow leaves make a very good first aid measure to stop bleeding. The fresh leaves can be can either be held or bound onto a wound. Call the vet if bleeding does not stop very quickly. Yarrow can also be used for steam inhalation for coughs.

St John's wort

(Hypericum perforatum)
Useful as a cream or ointment for wounds. This herb stimulates granulation tissue and therefore aids healing. However, horses are predisposed to the development of 'proud flesh', so use should therefore be cautious whenever this could be a problem. Oil can be used at the rate of 5 drops to 25ml of sunflower oil to massage inflamed joints and tendons.

Witch hazel

(Hamamelis virginiana)
This herb is widely available as distilled extract of witch hazel. A cold compress is used for wounds, especially if there is bruising. It is also used for insect bites.

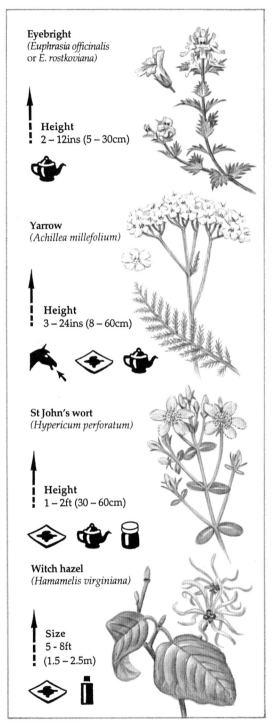

Eyebright
*(Euphrasia officinalis
or E. rostkoviana)*

Height
2 – 12ins (5 – 30cm)

Yarrow
(Achillea millefolium)

Height
3 – 24ins (8 – 60cm)

St John's wort
(Hypericum perforatum)

Height
1 – 2ft (30 – 60cm)

Witch hazel
(Hamamelis virginiana)

Size
5 - 8ft
(1.5 – 2.5m)

Herbal hints and tips

Mustard (paste) can be spread on stable doors and fences to deter crib-biting.

Leave a cut onion in the stable to keep flies away.

Oil of citronella is a cheap fly repellent. Either mix five drops with 500ml of grape seed or other thin oil or use neat, two drops on forelock and two drops on top of tail.

Used tea bags, chilled in the fridge, reduce eye swellings.

Lavender oil can be used on insect bites and stings, both to soothe the sting and to repel further attack.

Dried southernwood and lavender keep moths away from winter rugs.

Bach Flower Rescue Remedy - a few drops inside the bottom lip is said to calm a horse after a fright or accident, or before clipping, loading etc.

Plant African marigolds (*Tagetes*) around the stable yard to keep flies away.

Tea tree oil - a powerful bactericide and fungicide. Available as a proprietary oil, with many uses. Especially good for ringworm and thrush.

Henna (of an appropriate colour) can be safely used to dye white patches caused by old injuries.

Mix together 5ml cumin oil and 5ml of cinnamon oil. A few drops on your hand will help to catch a difficult horse.

Slippery elm (*Ulmus fulva*) makes a very good, and soothing, 'sticky' base to mix with other herbs for a poultice.

Making herbal preparations

Infusion: This is just like making a cup of tea. Use 30g dried or 75g fresh herb, add 250ml of almost boiling water and leave to brew for 10 minutes. Do not strain, unless you are drinking it yourself or using for bathing. When bathing an affected area, blot up excess moisture and leave to dry naturally.

Decoction: Use the same quantity of herbs, but 500ml of water. Boil for one hour. Strain.

Poultice: Chop fresh herbs (enough to cover area to be poulticed) or moisten dried herbs with hot water. Cut a sufficiently large piece of gamgee tissue and lay it on top of a similar sized piece of polythene. Spread the herbs on the gamgee and carefully pour over sufficient very hot water to soak. When cool enough to handle without burning, squeeze out any excess water and either bandage or hold onto the affected part. If bandaging onto a leg, leave in place for several hours or overnight. Leave off during the day and apply a fresh poultice the next evening if necessary. If holding onto the affected part, do so for as long as possible, every few hours, changing the poultice for a fresh one each time.

Compress: This is the 'liquid only', usually cold, version of a poultice. An infusion or decoction can be used, rather than the actual herb, as in a poultice. A cloth is wrung out in the solution and applied to the affected part. It can be bandaged onto a leg, and left on or held in place as for a poultice.

Cream: This is a cheap method of making your own cream. It works especially well with marigold petals. Melt 150g emulsifying ointment (bought from chemists) and 70ml glycerine in a double saucepan. Add 30g of dried herb and heat gently together for three hours. Strain and stir continually until cold. Store in refrigerator or cold place.

Oil: Essential oils are readily available in health food and similar shops. Add 4 – 5 drops of the essential oil to 500ml of sunflower or grape seed oil and use as indicated.

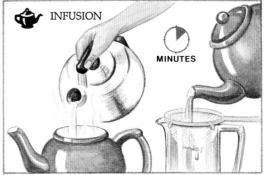

INFUSION

MINUTES

DECOCTION

HOURS

POULTICE

CREAM

HOURS